The Gold-Bug

Codes, Hidden Treasure & Clever Detective Work in a Seaside Mystery

A Modern Translation

Adapted for the Contemporary Reader

Edgar Allan Poe

Translated by Tim Zengerink

Table of Contents

Preface
Message to the Reader

Rebuilding the Greatest Library in Human History

Thousands of years ago, the Library of Alexandria was the heart of global knowledge — a sanctuary where the wisdom of every known civilization was gathered and shared freely.

And then, it was lost.

Now, we're rebuilding it — and you are invited to join us.

At the Library of Alexandria, we've set out to make every book available to every person on Earth — not just in print, but in every language, every format, and for every reader.

Here's how we do it:

- **Deluxe Print Editions at True Printing Cost** - Order any book as a high-quality paperback, elegant hardcover, or stunning boxset — and only pay what it costs to print. No markups. No middlemen.
- **Unlimited Access to the Greatest Works** - Enjoy thousands of timeless classics — from Plato to Shakespeare to Tolstoy — in beautiful, modern eBook and audiobook editions. Read and listen without limits — for every reader, everywhere.
- **Modern Translations for Every Language & Dialect** - We're reimagining the classics in clear, accessible language — and translating them into every dialect imaginable. Everyone deserves to understand humanity's greatest ideas.

When you visit **LibraryofAlexandria.com**, you're not just accessing books — you're joining a global movement to restore, preserve, and share the wisdom of civilization.

Join us today at LibraryofAlexandria.com

Together, we'll ensure the light of human wisdom never fades again.

With gratitude,

The Modern Library of Alexandria Team

Visit:
www.libraryofalexandria.com
Or scan the code below:

Introduction

Whilomville and the Social Landscape of Fear

Stephen Crane's *The Monster* (1898) stands as one of the most strikingly modern and unsettling works of 19th-century American fiction. Beneath its seemingly simple narrative—of a heroic Black coachman, Henry Johnson, who saves a white child from a burning house only to be disfigured and rejected by the very community he saved—lies a piercing exploration of race, fear, and social hypocrisy. Set in the fictional town of Whilomville, the novella dissects the undercurrents of small-town life, where appearances and conformity dictate moral judgments far more than justice, compassion, or gratitude.

Whilomville is both an ordinary and extraordinary place. On the surface, it mirrors countless American towns of the post-Civil War era, marked by racial segregation, unspoken codes of social conduct, and a rigid class structure. Yet Crane transforms this setting into an almost laboratory-like space where the collective psyche of a community is examined under stress. Henry Johnson's disfigurement and subsequent ostracism act as the catalyst for this moral experiment. The town's reaction to him exposes its latent fears: fear of the "Other," fear of deviation from social norms, and ultimately, fear of moral courage. Through vivid sketches of town gossip, whispered conversations, and cruel mockery, Crane creates a microcosm of the larger racial and social tensions that plagued America at the close of the 19th century.

At its heart, *The Monster* is a study of what it means to be human—and what it means to be dehumanized. Johnson's transformation from a familiar and respected figure into a "monster" in the eyes of the townspeople reveals the power of perception and prejudice. His sacrifice, which should elevate him to the status of hero, instead relegates him to that of a social outcast. Crane uses this paradox to interrogate the fragile nature of morality in a society that places superficial appearances above inner character. By doing so, he challenges the reader to confront uncomfortable truths about both the cruelty and cowardice that can emerge from collective judgment.

Themes of Race, Morality, and Social Hypocrisy

Race lies at the core of *The Monster.* Written during an era when Jim Crow laws were tightening across the United States, Crane's novella addresses the ways in which African Americans were both visible and invisible—present as laborers and servants, yet excluded from genuine social acceptance and equality. Henry Johnson is treated as a loyal servant and a dependable member of the Trescott household, but the moment he no longer fits the visual and social mold that the town demands, he is cast out. His disfigurement, compounded by his race, becomes an unbearable symbol of difference. For the white townspeople, he is no longer "one of them" but rather a being who defies their narrow definition of normalcy.

Crane does not shy away from portraying the venomous nature of small-town gossip and its ability to destroy lives. The townspeople's reaction to Dr. Trescott's decision to care for Johnson—shielding him from public mockery and providing for his needs—serves as a litmus test for Whilomville's moral fabric. Rather than applaud the doctor's compassion, the community turns on him, treating him and his family as accomplices to Johnson's "monstrous" presence. This reaction underscores one of Crane's most biting critiques: the ease with which communities sacrifice morality for the sake of maintaining social cohesion and appearances.

The figure of Dr. Trescott is central to the novella's moral discourse. His steadfast loyalty to Johnson, despite immense social pressure, highlights the cost of true ethical action in a conformist society. Trescott's character serves as a counterpoint to the town's collective cowardice; yet even his actions are tinged with complexity. Is his care for Johnson purely altruistic, or is it also driven by guilt, since Johnson's injuries were sustained while saving the doctor's own child? Crane refuses to give simple answers, instead presenting morality as a tangled web of motives, obligations, and consequences.

The title of the novella, *The Monster*, is itself a powerful irony. The real "monsters" in the story are not those who bear physical scars but those who allow fear and prejudice to corrupt their humanity. Johnson, though outwardly disfigured, remains the novella's most dignified and morally pure character, whereas the townspeople—unscarred but inwardly deformed by their bigotry—embody the true moral ugliness. In this inversion, Crane challenges readers to reconsider what it means to be monstrous.

Crane's Style and the Reader's Experience

To fully appreciate *The Monster*, one must pay attention to Crane's distinctive narrative style. Known for his journalistic precision and vivid impressionistic descriptions, Crane blends realism with symbolic undertones that deepen the novella's impact. His portrayal of Whilomville is detailed yet unsentimental; he paints the town's streets, porches, and gossiping circles with a reporter's eye for detail, while simultaneously imbuing the scenes with a sense of moral and psychological tension. The fire that disfigures Henry Johnson, for instance, is rendered in both literal and metaphorical terms, serving as a crucible that exposes the characters' inner values.

Crane's use of dialogue is another crucial element of the novella's realism. The townspeople's conversations, often laced with humor, sarcasm, or cruelty, reflect the rhythms of small-town speech while also serving as a chorus of collective opinion. These dialogues make the reader an eavesdropper, positioned to witness the social dynamics that drive the narrative forward. Through these moments, Crane captures how ordinary language can both reveal and reinforce prejudice.

One of Crane's greatest strengths is his ability to create empathy through understatement. He rarely preaches or moralizes; instead, he presents scenes and lets them speak for themselves. The sight of Henry Johnson hiding his ruined face beneath bandages, the Trescotts enduring silent stares and whispers, or the chilling laughter of children mocking the "monster"—these images carry a weight of emotion and judgment that no authorial commentary could surpass. Crane's restraint forces the reader to grapple with the story's ethical questions directly, without the buffer of narrative instruction.

For the modern reader, *The Monster* remains strikingly relevant. Issues of race, social exclusion, and moral courage continue to resonate in contemporary society. The novella's exploration of how communities treat those who are "different"—whether because of race, appearance, or other factors—has lost none of its power. In fact, the story's brevity and intensity make it all the more impactful; there is no padding or digression to dilute its central themes.

Approaching *The Monster* today, one should be prepared for both the historical specificity of Crane's setting and the timeless nature of his moral inquiry. The late 19th century was a period of deep racial tensions, with the promises of Reconstruction giving way to the harsh realities of segregation and systemic discrimination. Crane, though a white author from the North, confronted these realities with a clarity and courage that was unusual for his time. While some of his depictions may reflect the prejudices of the era, his overarching critique of social injustice remains powerful and unflinching.

To read *The Monster* is to be challenged. Crane asks us not only to consider the fate of Henry Johnson but also to reflect on our own communities, our own capacities for compassion or cruelty, and the ways in which fear can deform the human spirit. As you embark on this reading, allow yourself to step into Whilomville, to witness its whispers and silences, its acts of bravery and its failures of humanity. Crane's story is not just about a man who became a "monster" but about the monstrous potential that resides in all of us when we allow fear to triumph over empathy.

The Gold-Bug

Many years ago, I became close friends with a man named William Legrand. He came from an old Huguenot family and had once been wealthy, but a string of misfortunes had left him in poverty. To escape the humiliation that followed his financial ruin, he left New Orleans, the city where his ancestors had lived, and made his home on Sullivan's Island, near Charleston, South Carolina.

This island is quite unique. It's made up of little more than sea sand and stretches about three miles in length. At its widest point, it's no more than a quarter mile across. A barely visible creek separates it from the mainland, seeping through a wilderness of reeds and mud that serves as a favorite gathering place for marsh hens. The plant life, as you might expect, is sparse or at least stunted. You won't find any large trees here. Near the western end, where Fort Moultrie is located and where some shabby wooden buildings house summer refugees escaping Charleston's dust and fever, you can find the spiky palmetto. However, the entire island, except for this western tip and a strip of hard, white beach along the ocean, is blanketed with thick undergrowth of sweet myrtle, a plant highly valued by English gardeners. This shrub often grows fifteen to twenty feet tall here, creating an almost impenetrable thicket that fills the air with its sweet scent.

In the deepest part of this wooded area, close to the eastern or far end of the island, Legrand had constructed a small cabin where he was living when I first met him by pure chance. Our acquaintance quickly developed into friendship—there was much about this hermit that sparked curiosity and respect. I discovered he was well-educated, possessing remarkable mental abilities, but he suffered from a hatred of humanity and was prone to unpredictable shifts between passionate excitement and deep sadness. He owned many books but seldom read them. His main pastimes were hunting and fishing, or wandering along the shoreline and through the myrtle groves, searching for shells or insect specimens—his insect collection could have made even Swammerdam jealous. On these outings he was typically joined by an elderly Black man named Jupiter, who had been freed before the family's financial troubles began, but who couldn't be persuaded, whether through threats or promises, to give up what he saw as his duty to follow his young "Master Will" wherever he went. It's quite possible that Legrand's family members, believing him to be mentally unstable, had deliberately encouraged Jupiter's stubbornness as a way to watch over and protect their wayward relative.

The winters at Sullivan's Island's latitude are rarely very harsh, and during autumn it's truly unusual when a fire becomes necessary. Around mid-October of 18—, however, there came a day of extraordinary coldness. Just before the sun set, I made my way through the evergreen trees to my friend's cabin, which I hadn't visited in several weeks—I was living in Charleston at the time, nine miles away from the island, and the transportation options back and forth were much more limited than they are today. When I reached the cabin, I knocked as I always did, and when no one answered, I looked for the key in its usual hiding spot, unlocked the door, and stepped inside. A beautiful fire was burning brightly in the fireplace. This was unexpected and certainly welcome. I removed my overcoat, settled into an armchair beside the crackling logs, and waited patiently for my hosts to return.

Soon after dark they arrived and gave me the warmest welcome. Jupiter was grinning from ear to ear as he busily prepared some marsh-hens for supper. Legrand was experiencing one of his episodes—what else could I call them?—of passionate excitement. He had discovered an unknown bivalve that represented an entirely new genus, and beyond that, he had tracked down and captured, with Jupiter's help, a scarab beetle that he believed was completely new to science, though he wanted my expert opinion about it the following day.

"And why not tonight?" I asked, rubbing my hands over the fire, and wishing the whole tribe of beetles to the devil.

"Oh, if I had only known you were here!" Legrand exclaimed, "but it's been such a long time since I last saw you; and how could I have predicted that you would come to visit me on this particular night of all nights? When I was walking home, I ran into Lieutenant G——, from the fort, and quite foolishly, I let him borrow the bug; so it won't be possible for you to see it until morning. Stay here tonight, and I'll send Jup down to get it at sunrise. It's the most beautiful thing in existence!"

"What?—sunrise?"

"Nonsense! No—the bug. It's a brilliant gold color—about the size of a large hickory nut—with two jet black spots near one end of its back, and another spot, somewhat longer, at the other end. The antennae are—"

"There ain't no tin in him, Master Will, I keep telling you," Jupiter interrupted here; "the bug is a gold bug, solid, every bit of him, inside and all, except his wings—never felt such a heavy bug in my life."

"Well, suppose it is, Jup," Legrand replied, seeming to me somewhat more serious than the situation called for, "is that any reason for you to let the birds burn? The color"—here he turned to me—"is really almost enough to justify Jupiter's idea. You've never seen a more brilliant metallic shine than what the scales give off—but you can't judge this until tomorrow. In the meantime, I can give you some idea of the shape." After saying this, he sat down at a small table that had a pen and ink on it, but no paper. He searched for some in a drawer, but didn't find any.

"Don't worry about it," he finally said, "this will work just fine." He pulled a piece of what looked like very dirty paper from his vest pocket and made a rough sketch on it with his pen. While he worked on this, I stayed in my chair by the fire since I was still feeling cold. When he finished the drawing, he handed it to me without getting up. As I took it from him, we heard a loud growl followed by scratching sounds at the door. Jupiter went over and opened it, and a large Newfoundland dog that belonged to Legrand came bounding in, jumped up on my shoulders, and showered me with affection. The dog had always been friendly with me because I had paid him a lot of attention during my previous visits. After he calmed down from his excited greeting, I examined the paper, and honestly, I found myself quite confused by what my friend had drawn.

"Well!" I said, after looking at it for several minutes, "this is definitely a strange beetle, I have to admit: it's completely new to me: I've never seen anything like it before—unless it was a skull, or a death's-head—which it looks more like than anything else I've ever observed."

"A skull!" Legrand repeated. "Oh—yes—well, it does look somewhat like that on paper, certainly. Those two dark spots at the top resemble eyes, don't they? And that longer mark at the bottom looks like a mouth—and the overall shape is oval."

"Maybe you're right," I said, "but Legrand, I'm afraid you're not much of an artist. I'll have to wait until I can see the beetle myself before I can get any sense of what it actually looks like."

"Well, I'm not sure about that," he said, feeling somewhat irritated. "I draw reasonably well—or at least I should be able to—I've had excellent teachers, and I like to think I'm not completely incompetent."

"But my dear friend, you must be kidding," I said. "This is actually a pretty decent skull—in fact, I'd say it's an excellent skull, at least by ordinary standards for these kinds of anatomical specimens. Your beetle would have to be the strangest beetle in the world if it looks like this. We could create quite an exciting supernatural story based on this idea. I suppose you'd name the bug scarabæus caput hominis, or something along those lines—there are many similar names in the Natural Histories. But where are the antennae you mentioned?"

"The antennae!" said Legrand, who seemed to be getting inexplicably excited about the subject; "I am sure you must see the antennae. I made them as clear as they are in the original insect, and I assume that is sufficient."

"Well, well," I said, "perhaps you have—still I don't see them;" and I handed him the paper without additional comment, not wanting to upset him; but I was very surprised at how things had developed; his bad mood confused me—and, as for the drawing of the beetle, there were definitely no antennae visible, and the whole thing did look very much like the typical illustrations of a death's-head.

He took the paper with obvious irritation and was about to crumple it up, apparently planning to toss it into the fire, when a quick look at the design suddenly captured his complete attention. Instantly his face turned bright red—then just as quickly became extremely pale. For several minutes he continued to examine the drawing closely while remaining seated. Eventually he stood up, grabbed a candle from the table, and went to sit on a sea chest in the far corner of the room. There he conducted another careful examination of the paper, rotating it in every direction. He said nothing, though, and his behavior greatly surprised me; still, I thought it wise not to worsen his increasingly dark mood with any remarks. Soon he pulled a wallet from his coat pocket, placed the paper carefully inside it, and put both items in a writing desk, which he then locked. He became calmer in his manner after this, but his initial enthusiasm had completely vanished. However, he appeared more lost in thought than sullen. As the evening progressed he became increasingly absorbed in deep contemplation, and nothing I said could snap him out of it. I had planned to spend the night at the cabin, as I had done many times before, but seeing my host in this state, I decided it would be best to leave. He didn't urge me to stay, but when I left, he shook my hand with even greater warmth than usual.

About a month later (during which time I hadn't seen Legrand at all), I received a visit in Charleston from his servant, Jupiter. I had never seen the good old man look so dejected, and I worried that some terrible misfortune had happened to my friend.

"Well, Jup," I said, "what's wrong now? How is your master?"

"Well, to tell the truth, master, he's not doing as well as he could be."

"Not well! I'm really sorry to hear that. What is he complaining about?"

"There! That's it!—he never complains about anything—but he's very sick despite all that."

"Very sick, Jupiter! Why didn't you say so right away? Is he stuck in bed?"

"No, he isn't!—he isn't to be found anywhere—that's exactly where the problem lies—my mind has become very heavy with worry about poor Master Will."

"Jupiter, I'd like to understand what you're talking about. You say your master is sick. Hasn't he told you what's wrong with him?"

"Why, master, it's not worth getting upset about this situation—Master Will says nothing at all is wrong with him—but then what makes him go around looking like this, with his head down and his shoulders hunched up, and as white as a ghost? And then he keeps sighing all the time—"

"Keeps a what, Jupiter?"

"He keeps a siphon with figures on the slate—the strangest figures I've ever seen. I'm getting scared, I tell you. I have to keep a very close eye on him always. The other day he gave me the slip before sunrise and was gone the whole blessed day. I had a big stick ready cut to give him a really good beating when he came back—but I'm such a fool that I didn't have the heart after all—he looked so very poorly."

"Huh? What? Oh yes! Overall, I think you shouldn't be too harsh with the poor guy—don't beat him, Jupiter—he can't handle it very well—but can't you think of anything that might have caused this sickness, or rather this change in behavior? Has anything upsetting happened since I last saw you?"

"No, sir, there hasn't been anything unpleasant since then—it was before then that I was afraid—it was the very day you were there."

"How? What do you mean?"

"Why, master, I mean the bug—there now."

"The what?"

"The bug—I'm absolutely certain that Master Will has been bitten somewhere around the head by that gold-bug."

"And what reason do you have, Jupiter, for making such an assumption?"

"It has enough claws, master, and a mouth too. I never did see such a terrible bug—it kicks and bites everything that comes near it. Master Will caught it first, but had to let it go again mighty quick, I tell you—then was the time it must have gotten the bite. I didn't like the look of the bug's mouth myself, no way, so I wouldn't take hold of it with my finger, but I caught it with a piece of paper that I found. I wrapped it up in the paper and stuffed a piece of it in its mouth—that was the way."

"And you think, then, that your master was really bitten by the beetle, and that the bite made him sick?"

"I don't think anything about it—I know it. What makes him dream about the gold so much, if it isn't because he's been bitten by the gold-bug? I've heard about those gold-bugs before this."

"But how do you know he dreams about gold?"

"How do I know? Well, because he talks about it in his sleep—that's how I know."

"Well, Jup, perhaps you are right; but what fortunate circumstance do I have to thank for the honor of a visit from you today?"

"What's the matter, master?"

"Did you bring any message from Mr. Legrand?"

"No, sir, I brought this letter;" and here Jupiter handed me a note which read as follows:

"MY DEAR ——

Why haven't I seen you for such a long time? I hope you haven't been foolish enough to take offense at some small rudeness on my part; but no, that's unlikely. Since I last saw you, I've had serious reasons to worry. I have something to tell you, but I hardly know how to say it, or whether I should say it at all.

"I haven't been feeling well for the past few days, and poor old Jup irritates me almost beyond what I can bear with his well-intentioned care. Can you believe it? The other day, he had prepared a large stick to punish me for escaping from him and spending the day alone among the hills on the mainland. I truly believe that my sickly appearance alone saved me from a beating."

"I haven't added anything to my collection since we last met."

"If you can manage it in any way, please come over with Jupiter. Do come. I need to see you tonight about important business. I assure you that it is of the highest importance."

Ever yours,

WILLIAM LEGRAND.

Something about the tone of this note filled me with deep concern. The entire style was completely different from Legrand's usual way of writing. What could he be thinking about? What strange new idea had taken hold of his restless mind? What kind of "business of the highest importance" could he possibly need to handle? Jupiter's description of him didn't sound promising at all. I was afraid that the ongoing weight of bad luck had finally driven my friend to lose his sanity. Without hesitating for even a moment, I got ready to go with the negro.

Upon reaching the dock, I saw a scythe and three shovels, all seemingly new, lying in the bottom of the boat we were about to board.

"What does all this mean, Jup?" I asked.

"Him syfe, massa, and spade."

"Very true; but what are they doing here?"

"The scythe and the spade that Master Will told me to buy for him in town, and I had to pay a devil of a lot of money for them."

"But what on earth is your 'Massa Will' planning to do with scythes and spades?"

"That's more than I know, and the devil take me if I don't believe it's more than he knows, too. But it's all come of the bug."

Finding that no satisfaction could be obtained from Jupiter, whose entire mind seemed to be consumed by "the bug," I now stepped into the boat and set sail. With a favorable and strong breeze we quickly sailed into the small cove north of Fort Moultrie, and a walk of approximately two miles brought us to the cabin. It was around three in the afternoon when we arrived. Legrand had been waiting for us with eager anticipation. He seized my hand with a nervous intensity that alarmed me and reinforced the suspicions I already harbored. His face was pale to the point of being ghostly, and his deep-set eyes blazed with an unnatural brightness. After some questions regarding his health, I asked him, not knowing what else to say, whether he had yet obtained the beetle from Lieutenant G——.

"Oh, yes," he replied, his face turning bright red, "I got it from him the next morning. Nothing could convince me to give up that beetle. Do you know that Jupiter is absolutely right about it?"

"How so?" I asked, feeling a heavy sense of dread in my heart.

"In assuming it was a bug made of real gold." He spoke with an air of deep seriousness, and I felt incredibly shocked.

"This bug is going to make me rich," he continued with a triumphant smile, "and restore me to my family's wealth. Is it any surprise, then, that I treasure it? Since Fortune has decided to give it to me, I only need to use it correctly and I'll find the gold it points to. Jupiter, bring me that beetle!"

"What! The bug, master? I'd rather not go looking for trouble with that bug—you must get it yourself." At this, Legrand stood up with a serious and dignified manner, and brought me the beetle from a glass case where it was kept. It was a beautiful scarab, and at that time, it was unknown to scientists—naturally a great discovery from a scientific perspective. There were two round, black spots near one end of its back, and a long one near the other end. The scales were extremely hard and shiny, with all the appearance of polished gold. The weight of the insect was very unusual, and considering everything, I could hardly fault Jupiter for his opinion about it; but what to make of Legrand's agreement with that opinion, I couldn't figure out to save my life.

"I called for you," he said in a pompous tone, after I had finished examining the beetle, "I called for you so that I could get your advice and help in advancing the plans of Fate and of the bug—"

"My dear Legrand," I exclaimed, cutting him off, "you're definitely not well, and you should take some precautions. You need to go to bed, and I'll stay with you for a few days until you recover. You have a fever and—"

"Check my pulse," he said.

I felt it, and to be honest, found no sign of fever whatsoever.

"But you might be sick even without running a fever. Let me give you medical advice just this once. First, you need to go to bed. Next—"

"You're wrong," he interrupted, "I'm doing as well as anyone could expect given the stress I'm dealing with. If you truly care about my wellbeing, you'll help ease this tension."

"And how is this to be done?"

"Very easily. Jupiter and I are going on an expedition into the hills on the mainland, and for this expedition we'll need help from someone we can trust completely. You're the only person we can rely on. Whether we succeed or fail, the excitement you see in me right now will be put to rest either way."

"I'm eager to help you in any way I can," I replied; "but are you telling me that this cursed beetle has something to do with your trip into the hills?"

"It has."

"Then, Legrand, I can't be part of such a ridiculous plan."

"I'm sorry—truly sorry—because we'll have to attempt this on our own."

"Try it yourselves! The man has clearly lost his mind!—but wait!—how long do you plan to be away?"

"Probably all night. We'll leave right away and be back by sunrise at the latest."

"And will you promise me, on your honor, that when this strange obsession of yours is finished, and the bug matter (good God!) resolved to your satisfaction, you will then come home and follow my advice completely, as that of your doctor?"

"Yes, I promise. Now let's go—we don't have any time to waste."

With a heavy heart, I went along with my friend. We set out around four o'clock—Legrand, Jupiter, the dog, and myself. Jupiter carried the scythe and shovels with him—all of which he insisted on carrying himself—more out of fear, it seemed to me, of letting either tool get within his master's reach than from any extra effort or eagerness to please. His attitude was extremely stubborn, and "dat deuced bug" were the only words that came out of his mouth during the trip. As for me, I was responsible for carrying a couple of dark lanterns, while Legrand satisfied himself with the beetle, which he had tied to the end of a piece of whip-cord, spinning it back and forth with the flair of a magician as he walked. When I noticed this final, clear proof of my friend's mental disturbance, I could barely hold back my tears. I decided it was best, though, to go along with his whim, at least for now, or until I could take some stronger action with a real chance of working. Meanwhile, I tried, but completely failed, to get him to tell me what the purpose of this expedition was. Having managed to convince me to come with him, he seemed reluctant to discuss any topic of lesser significance, and to all my questions he gave no other answer than "we shall see!"

We crossed the creek at the head of the island using a small boat, and after climbing the high ground on the mainland shore, we continued in a northwesterly direction through an extremely wild and desolate stretch of countryside where no sign of human presence could be found. Legrand led the way with confidence, stopping only briefly now and then to check what seemed to be specific landmarks he had created on a previous visit.

We traveled this way for about two hours, and the sun was just setting when we entered a region far more desolate than anything we had seen before. It was a kind of plateau, near the top of an almost unreachable hill, thickly forested from bottom to peak, and scattered with enormous rocks that seemed to rest loosely on the ground, and in many instances were kept from tumbling into the valleys below only by the trees they leaned against. Deep gorges, running in different directions, gave the scene an even more forbidding solemnity.

The natural ledge we had climbed up to was completely covered with thick brambles, and we quickly realized it would have been impossible to push through them without the scythe; Jupiter, following his master's instructions, began cutting a path for us toward the base of an incredibly tall tulip tree that stood alongside eight or ten oak trees on the flat ground, and it far exceeded all of them, as well as every other tree I had ever seen at that time, in the stunning beauty of its leaves and shape, in the vast reach of its branches, and in the overall magnificence of its presence. When we reached this tree, Legrand turned to Jupiter and asked him whether he thought he could climb it. The old man appeared somewhat taken aback by the question, and for several moments he didn't respond. Finally he walked up to the massive trunk, moved slowly around it, and studied it with careful attention. After he had finished his examination, he simply said,

"Yes, master, Jupiter can climb any tree he's ever seen in his life."

"Then get up as quickly as you can, because it will soon be too dark to see what we're doing."

"How far should I go up, master?" Jupiter asked.

"Climb up the main trunk first, and then I'll tell you which direction to go—and here—wait! Take this beetle with you."

"The bug, Master Will! The gold bug!" cried the man, pulling back in alarm. "Why do I have to carry the bug all the way up the tree? I'll be damned if I do!"

"If you're scared, Jup, a big strong man like you, to pick up a harmless little dead beetle, then you can carry it up using this string—but if you don't take it with you somehow, I'll have no choice but to crack your head with this shovel."

"What's the matter now, sir?" said Jupiter, clearly embarrassed into cooperating; "always wanting to make trouble with this old man. I was just joking around anyway. Me afraid of the bug! Why would I care about the bug?" Here he carefully grabbed the very end of the string, and keeping the insect as far away from himself as possible, got ready to climb the tree.

When young, the tulip tree, or Liriodendron Tulipferum, which is the most magnificent tree in American forests, has a trunk that is remarkably smooth and often grows to great heights without any side branches; however, as it matures, the bark becomes rough and uneven, while numerous short branches begin to appear along the trunk. Therefore, the challenge of climbing it in this particular situation was more apparent than real. Wrapping his arms and knees around the massive trunk as tightly as he could, gripping various bumps and ridges with his hands while placing his bare toes on others, Jupiter, after nearly falling once or twice, finally managed to work his way up to the first major fork in the tree and seemed to feel that he had essentially completed the task. The dangerous part of this feat was actually finished now, even though the climber was still sixty or seventy feet above the ground.

"Which way should we go now, Master Will?" he asked.

"Keep climbing the biggest branch—the one on this side," Legrand said. The man obeyed him quickly and seemingly with little difficulty, climbing higher and higher until his stocky figure could no longer be seen through the thick leaves that surrounded him. Soon his voice could be heard calling out.

"How much further do we have to go?"

"How high up are you?" asked Legrand.

"Even farther," replied the man; "I can see the sky through the top of the tree."

"Don't worry about the sky, just listen to what I'm telling you. Look down the trunk and count the branches below you on this side. How many branches have you gone past?"

"One, two, three, four, five—I have passed five big limbs, master, on this side."

"Then climb up one branch higher."

In just a few minutes, the voice could be heard once more, declaring that the seventh limb had been reached.

"Now, Jup," Legrand called out, clearly very excited, "I need you to crawl out on that branch as far as you can go. If you notice anything unusual, tell me right away." At this point, any remaining doubts I might have had about my poor friend's mental state were completely eliminated. I had no choice but to believe he had lost his mind, and I grew genuinely worried about how to get him back home. While I was thinking about the best course of action, we heard Jupiter's voice once more.

"I'm afraid to venture out on this limb very far—it's a dead limb pretty much all the way."

"Did you say it was a dead branch, Jupiter?" Legrand called out in a trembling voice.

"Yes, master, he's dead as a doornail—finished for certain—he's departed this life."

"What on earth am I supposed to do?" asked Legrand, appearing to be in tremendous distress.

"Do it!" I said, happy to finally get a chance to jump into the conversation. "Why don't you just go home and get some sleep? Come on now—be a good sport about it. It's getting late, and don't forget, you made a promise."

"Jupiter," he shouted, completely ignoring me, "can you hear me?"

"Yes, Master Will, I can hear you very clearly."

"Test the wood thoroughly with your knife, then, and see if you think it's very rotten."

"He's rotten, master, that's for sure," the man replied after a few moments, "but not as completely rotten as he could be. I might be able to venture out a little way on the limb by myself, that's true."

"By yourself!—what do you mean?"

"I mean the bug. It's a very heavy bug. Suppose I drop it down first, and then the branch won't break with just the weight of one person."

"You absolute rascal!" Legrand shouted, clearly feeling much better, "what's the point of telling me such ridiculous nonsense? I swear, if you drop that beetle, I'll break your neck. Listen here, Jupiter, are you hearing me?"

"Yes, sir, you don't need to yell at me like that."

"Alright! Now listen carefully—if you're willing to crawl out on that branch as far as you think is safe, and make sure you don't drop the beetle, I'll give you a silver dollar the moment you climb back down."

"I'm going, Master Will—indeed I am," replied the negro very promptly—"almost out to the end now."

"All the way to the end!" Legrand practically screamed at this point, "are you telling me you're out at the very end of that branch?"

"It'll be over soon, master—oh-oh-oh-oh! Lord have mercy! What is that there on the tree?"

"Well!" exclaimed Legrand, absolutely thrilled, "what is it?"

"There's nothing there but a skull—someone left their head up in the tree, and the crows have eaten every bit of meat off it."

"A skull, you say! Very well—how is it attached to the limb? What keeps it in place?"

"That's right, master; must take a look. Why, this is a very curious circumstance, upon my word—there's a great big nail in the skull that fastens it to the tree."

"Listen, Jupiter, do exactly what I'm telling you—do you understand?"

"Yes, sir."

"Pay attention, then—find the left eye of the skull."

"Hmm! Whoa! That's good! Why, there isn't any eye left at all."

"Damn your foolishness! Do you even know your right hand from your left?"

"Yes, I know that—I know all about that—it's my left hand that I chop the wood with."

"Absolutely! You're left-handed, and your left eye is on the same side as your left hand. Now, I imagine you can locate the left eye socket of the skull, or the spot where the left eye used to be. Have you found it?"

Here was a long pause. Eventually the Black man asked,

"Is the left eye of the skull on the same side as the left hand of the skull, too?—because the skull doesn't have even a bit of a hand at all—never mind! I found the left eye now—here's the left eye! What should I do with it?"

"Let the beetle fall through it as far as the string allows—but be careful not to let go of your grip on the string."

"All that's done, Master Will; it's really easy to put the bug through the hole—watch out for it down there below!"

During this conversation, no part of Jupiter's body could be seen; but the beetle, which he had allowed to descend, was now visible at the end of the string, and gleamed like a sphere of polished gold in the final rays of the setting sun, some of which still dimly lit the hill where we stood. The beetle hung completely free of any branches, and if dropped, would have landed at our feet. Legrand immediately grabbed the scythe and used it to clear a circular area, three or four yards across, directly beneath the insect, and after finishing this task, told Jupiter to release the string and climb down from the tree.

Carefully driving a peg into the ground at the exact spot where the beetle had fallen, my friend pulled a tape measure from his pocket. He attached one end to the part of the tree trunk closest to the peg, then unrolled the tape until it reached the peg, and continued unrolling it in the direction established by the tree and peg for a distance of fifty feet—with Jupiter clearing away the thorny bushes using his scythe. At this new location, he drove in a second peg, and using it as the center point, he marked out a rough circle about four feet across. Legrand then picked up a spade for himself and handed one to Jupiter and another to me, urging us to begin digging as quickly as we could.

To be honest, I had no particular enthusiasm for this kind of entertainment at any time, and at that specific moment, I would have gladly avoided it; the night was approaching, and I felt quite tired from the physical activity we had already undertaken; however, I could see no way to get out of it, and I was afraid of upsetting my poor friend's peace of mind by refusing. If I could have counted on Jupiter's help, I would not have hesitated to try forcing the madman home; but I knew the old man's character too well to hope that he would help me, under any circumstances, in a physical struggle with his master. I had no doubt that his master had been influenced by some of the countless Southern superstitions about buried treasure, and that his delusion had been strengthened by discovering the scarab, or perhaps by Jupiter's stubbornness in insisting it was "a bug of real gold." A mind inclined toward madness would easily be swayed by such ideas—especially if they matched cherished beliefs he already held—and then I remembered the poor man's words about the beetle being "the index of his fortune." Overall, I was deeply frustrated and confused, but eventually, I decided to make the best of a bad situation—to dig enthusiastically, and thereby convince the dreamer more quickly, through clear evidence, that his beliefs were false.

Once the lanterns were lit, we all began working with an enthusiasm that would have been better suited to a more sensible purpose; and as the light illuminated our faces and tools, I couldn't help but think about what a striking scene we created, and how odd and questionable our activities would have seemed to any outsider who might have accidentally discovered our location.

We dug steadily for two hours without stopping. We didn't say much during this time, and our main problem was the dog's constant barking as he showed intense interest in what we were doing. Eventually, he became so disruptive that we started worrying he might alert any wanderers who happened to be nearby—or at least, this was Legrand's concern. As for me, I would have welcomed any interruption that could have given me a chance to get this eccentric man back home. Jupiter finally put an end to the noise quite effectively by climbing out of the hole with a stubborn, deliberate manner, using one of his suspenders to tie the animal's mouth shut, and then returning to his work with a serious chuckle.

When the allotted time had passed, we had dug down five feet deep, but still no signs of treasure appeared. Everyone stopped digging, and I started to hope this whole charade was finally over. However, Legrand, though clearly frustrated, wiped the sweat from his forehead thoughtfully and started digging again. We had dug out the entire circle that was four feet across, and now we made it a bit wider and went down another two feet. Still, nothing showed up. The treasure hunter, whom I genuinely felt sorry for, finally climbed out of the hole with bitter disappointment written all over his face, and slowly and reluctantly began putting his coat back on, which he had taken off when he first started working. Meanwhile, I didn't say anything. Jupiter, following a gesture from his master, started collecting his tools. Once that was finished and the dog's muzzle had been removed, we headed home in complete silence.

We had walked maybe a dozen steps in that direction when Legrand suddenly cursed loudly, strode up to Jupiter, and grabbed him by the collar. The startled man's eyes and mouth opened wide, he dropped the shovels, and fell to his knees.

"You scoundrel," said Legrand, hissing the words through his clenched teeth—"you damned villain!—speak up, I'm telling you!—answer me right now, without beating around the bush!—which—which is your left eye?"

"Oh my goodness, Master Will! Isn't this my left eye for certain?" shouted the terrified Jupiter, placing his hand over his right eye and holding it there with desperate determination, as if he was immediately afraid his master might try to gouge it out.

"I thought so!—I knew it! hurrah!" shouted Legrand, releasing the black man and performing a series of leaps and spins, much to the amazement of his servant, who, getting up from his knees, looked silently from his master to me, and then from me back to his master.

"Come! We have to go back," he said, "the game isn't over yet;" and once again he led the way to the tulip tree.

"Jupiter," he said when we reached the base of the tree, "come here! Was the skull nailed to the branch with the face pointing outward, or with the face turned toward the branch?"

"The face was exposed, master, so that the crows could easily reach the eyes without any difficulty."

"Well, then, was it this eye or that one you dropped the beetle through?"—here Legrand touched each of Jupiter's eyes.

"'It was this eye, master—the left eye—just as you told me," and here it was his right eye that the man indicated.

"That will do—we must try it again."

Here my friend, whose madness I now noticed, or thought I noticed, showed certain signs of having a plan, moved the peg that marked where the beetle had fallen to a spot roughly three inches west of where it had been before. He then took the tape measure from the closest point of the tree trunk to the peg, just as he had done earlier, and extended it in a straight line for fifty feet, which indicated a spot that was several yards away from the point where we had been digging.

Around the new position, we drew a circle that was somewhat larger than the previous one, and we started working with our shovels again. I was terribly tired, but without really understanding what had caused this shift in my thinking, I no longer felt such strong resistance to the work we had to do. I had become inexplicably interested—even excited, in fact. Perhaps there was something in all of Legrand's eccentric behavior—some sense of planning or careful thought that made an impression on me. I dug with enthusiasm, and occasionally found myself actually searching with what closely resembled anticipation for the imagined treasure that had driven my unfortunate friend to madness. Just when these wandering thoughts had completely taken hold of me, and when we had been working for about an hour and a half, the dog's violent howling interrupted us once more. His restlessness at first had clearly been nothing more than playful mischief, but now his tone became harsh and serious. When Jupiter tried to muzzle him again, the dog fought back fiercely and jumped into the hole, frantically clawing at the dirt with his paws. Within moments, he had exposed a collection of human bones that formed two complete skeletons, mixed together with several metal buttons and what looked like the remains of rotted wool fabric. A stroke or two of the shovel revealed the blade of a large Spanish knife, and as we continued digging, three or four loose gold and silver coins emerged into the light.

When Jupiter saw these, his joy was almost impossible to contain, but his master's face showed deep disappointment. Nevertheless, he encouraged us to keep working, and he had barely finished speaking when I tripped and tumbled forward, catching the toe of my boot on a large iron ring that was partially buried in the loose soil.

We now worked with serious determination, and I had never experienced ten minutes of such intense excitement. During this time we had completely uncovered a rectangular wooden chest, which, judging by its perfect condition and remarkable hardness, had clearly undergone some kind of mineralizing treatment—possibly involving mercury bichloride. This chest measured three and a half feet in length, three feet in width, and two and a half feet in depth. It was securely fastened with bands of wrought iron that were riveted together, creating a kind of open lattice pattern across the entire surface. On each side of the chest, positioned near the top, were three iron rings—making six total—which would allow six people to get a solid grip. Even with all of us working together as hard as we could, we only managed to shift the chest very slightly from where it rested. We immediately realized it would be impossible to move something so heavy. Fortunately, the lid was held in place by just two sliding bolts. We pulled these back—our hands shaking and our hearts pounding with anticipation. In that moment, a treasure of immeasurable worth lay sparkling before our eyes. As the light from our lanterns shone down into the pit, a brilliant glow and radiance burst upward from a jumbled pile of gold and jewels that completely overwhelmed our vision.

I won't try to describe the emotions I felt as I stared at the scene. Amazement was certainly the strongest feeling. Legrand looked completely drained from all the excitement and barely spoke a word. For several minutes, Jupiter's face showed the kind of deathly pale color that was as extreme as possible for a Black man's complexion to display. He appeared stunned—as if struck by lightning. Soon he dropped to his knees in the pit and buried his bare arms up to his elbows in the gold, leaving them there as if he were enjoying a luxurious bath. Finally, with a deep sigh, he cried out as if talking to himself:

"And this all came from the gold-bug! The pretty gold-bug! The poor little gold-bug that I treated in such a savage way! Aren't you ashamed of yourself?—answer me that!"

Eventually, I realized that both my master and his servant needed to understand how important it was to move the treasure. Time was running out, and we had to work quickly to get everything safely stored before sunrise. We struggled to decide what to do, spending far too much time discussing our options—everyone's thoughts were jumbled and unclear. Finally, we made the box lighter by taking out two-thirds of what was inside, which allowed us to lift it out of the hole, though it still took considerable effort. We hid the items we had removed among the thorny bushes and left the dog to watch over them, with Jupiter giving him strict instructions not to move from that spot for any reason and to keep quiet until we came back. We then rushed home carrying the chest, managing to reach the cabin safely, though completely exhausted, at one o'clock in the morning. As tired as we were, it was impossible for anyone to do more work right away. We rested until two o'clock and ate supper, then immediately headed back to the hills, bringing along three sturdy sacks that we were fortunate to have at the cabin. Just before four o'clock, we reached the pit, divided up the remaining treasure as evenly as we could among ourselves, and left the holes unfilled as we set out once again for the cabin, where we stored our golden treasure for the second time, just as the first pale light of dawn began to appear above the treetops in the east.

We were completely exhausted by this point, but the overwhelming excitement of the moment wouldn't let us rest. After a restless sleep that lasted only three or four hours, we got up as if we had planned it together to examine our treasure.

The chest was completely full, and we spent the entire day and most of the following night carefully examining everything inside. Nothing had been organized or arranged in any particular way. Everything was just piled together randomly. After we carefully sorted through all the items, we discovered we possessed even greater wealth than we had initially thought. In coins alone, there was more than four hundred and fifty thousand dollars—we calculated the value of each piece as precisely as possible using the currency tables from that time period. There wasn't a single piece of silver. Everything was gold from ancient times and showed incredible variety—French, Spanish, and German currency, along with a few English guineas, and some tokens we had never encountered before. Several coins were extremely large and heavy, but they were so worn down that we couldn't make out any of the writing on them. There was no American currency. We had much more trouble determining the value of the jewels. There were diamonds—some incredibly large and of exceptional quality—one hundred and ten total, and every single one was substantial in size; eighteen rubies with extraordinary brilliance; three hundred and ten emeralds, all stunning; and twenty-one sapphires, plus one opal. All these precious stones had been removed from their original settings and were scattered loose throughout the chest. The settings themselves, which we gathered from among the other gold pieces, looked like they had been smashed with hammers, apparently to make them impossible to identify. Beyond all this, there was an enormous amount of solid gold jewelry; nearly two hundred heavy finger rings and earrings; expensive chains—thirty of them, if my memory serves me correctly; eighty-three very large and weighty crucifixes; five valuable gold incense burners; an enormous golden punch bowl decorated with intricately carved vine leaves and figures from Bacchanalian celebrations; two sword handles with exquisite embossed designs, and many other smaller items that I can't remember. The total weight of these precious objects was more than three hundred and fifty pounds; and this calculation doesn't even include one hundred and ninety-seven magnificent gold watches; three of them were each worth at least five hundred dollars. Many were extremely old and completely useless for telling time; their internal mechanisms had been damaged to varying degrees by rust and corrosion—but all were richly decorated with jewels and housed in cases of tremendous value. That night, we estimated the total contents of the chest at one and a half million dollars; and when we later sold the trinkets and jewels (keeping just a few for ourselves), we realized we had significantly underestimated the value of the treasure.

When we finally finished our examination and the intense excitement of the moment had somewhat calmed down, Legrand, who could see that I was desperately eager for an explanation of this most extraordinary mystery, began to provide a complete account of all the circumstances surrounding it.

"You remember," he said, "the night when I gave you the rough sketch I had drawn of the beetle. You also recall that I became quite annoyed with you for insisting that my drawing looked like a skull. When you first made this claim, I thought you were joking; but later I remembered the distinctive markings on the insect's back, and I admitted to myself that your comment had some basis in reality. Still, the mockery of my artistic abilities irritated me—since I'm considered a skilled artist—and so when you handed me that piece of parchment, I was about to crumple it up and angrily throw it into the fire."

"You're talking about that piece of paper," I said.

"No; it looked very much like paper, and at first I thought that's what it was, but when I started to draw on it, I immediately realized it was actually a piece of very thin parchment. It was quite dirty, as you'll recall. Well, just as I was about to crumple it up, my eyes fell on the sketch you had been examining, and you can imagine my shock when I saw what was clearly the figure of a death's-head right where I thought I had drawn the beetle. For a moment I was too stunned to think clearly. I knew my drawing was very different in its details from this—though there was some similarity in the general shape. I quickly grabbed a candle and sat down at the far end of the room to examine the parchment more carefully. When I flipped it over, I saw my own sketch on the back, exactly as I had drawn it. My first reaction was simply amazement at the truly extraordinary similarity of the outlines—at the strange coincidence that, without my knowledge, there had been a skull on the other side of the parchment, directly beneath my drawing of the beetle, and that this skull matched my drawing so closely, not just in outline but in size as well. I must say the strangeness of this coincidence completely bewildered me for a while. This is what such coincidences typically do. The mind tries to find a connection—some chain of cause and effect—and when it can't, it experiences a kind of temporary paralysis. But when I snapped out of this daze, a realization gradually came over me that shocked me even more than the coincidence itself. I began clearly and definitely to remember that there had been no drawing on the parchment when I sketched the beetle. I became absolutely certain of this, because I remembered examining first one side and then the other, looking for the cleanest area. If the skull had been there then, I certainly would have noticed it. Here was truly a mystery that seemed impossible to solve; but even at that early moment, there seemed to flicker dimly in the deepest, most hidden corners of my mind, a firefly-like glimpse of that truth which last night's adventure would so brilliantly reveal. I stood up immediately and carefully put the parchment away, putting off any further thought about it until I could be alone.

"After you left, and once Jupiter had fallen into a deep sleep, I began a more systematic examination of the situation. First, I thought about how the parchment had come into my hands. The location where we found the scarab beetle was along the mainland coast, roughly a mile east of the island, just a short way above the high tide line. When I grabbed it, the beetle gave me a sharp bite that made me drop it immediately. Jupiter, being naturally careful, looked around for a leaf or something similar to pick up the insect with before catching it as it flew toward him. At that exact moment, both his eyes and mine spotted the piece of parchment, which I initially thought was just paper. It lay partially buried in the sand with one corner poking out. Close to where we discovered it, I noticed the remains of what looked like it had once been a ship's longboat hull. The wreckage appeared to have been there for an extremely long time, as you could barely make out that the pieces had once been boat timber."

"Well, Jupiter picked up the parchment, wrapped the beetle in it, and handed it to me. Shortly after that, we started heading home, and along the way we ran into Lieutenant G——. I showed him the insect, and he asked if he could take it back to the fort. When I agreed, he immediately stuffed it into his vest pocket, leaving behind the parchment it had been wrapped in, which I was still holding during his examination. Maybe he was worried I might change my mind and figured it was better to secure his prize right away—you know how passionate he gets about anything related to Natural History. At the same time, without realizing it, I must have slipped the parchment into my own pocket.

"You remember that when I went to the table to sketch the beetle, I couldn't find any paper where it was normally kept. I looked through the drawer and found nothing there. I searched my pockets, hoping to discover an old letter, when my hand came across the parchment. I'm explaining exactly how it came into my possession because the circumstances struck me as particularly significant."

"You'll probably think I'm being imaginative—but I had already made a kind of connection. I had linked together two pieces of a great chain. There was a boat lying on a seacoast, and not far from the boat was a parchment—not a paper—with a skull drawn on it. You will, of course, ask 'where is the connection?' I answer that the skull, or death's-head, is the well-known symbol of the pirate. The flag of the death's head is raised in all battles."

"I mentioned that the scrap was made of parchment, not paper. Parchment lasts a long time—it's nearly indestructible. Important matters are rarely written on parchment because for ordinary drawing or writing, it doesn't work nearly as well as paper. This thought made me think the skull symbol had some meaning—some significance. I also noticed the shape of the parchment. Even though one corner had been damaged by accident, I could tell the original shape was rectangular. It was exactly the kind of piece someone might choose for a note—for recording something meant to be remembered for a long time and kept safe."

"But," I interrupted, "you say that the skull wasn't on the parchment when you made the drawing of the beetle. How then do you trace any connection between the boat and the skull—since this latter, according to your own admission, must have been designed (God only knows how or by whom) at some period after you sketched the scarab?"

"Ah, this is where the entire mystery revolves; though at this stage, I found the secret relatively easy to figure out. My reasoning was solid and could only lead to one conclusion. I thought it through like this: When I sketched the beetle, there was no skull visible on the parchment. After I finished the drawing, I handed it to you and watched you closely until you gave it back. Therefore, you didn't draw the skull, and nobody else was there to create it. So it wasn't made by human hands. Yet somehow, it appeared anyway.

"At this point in my thoughts, I tried to recall, and did recall with complete clarity, every detail that happened during that particular time. The weather was cold (what a rare and fortunate coincidence!), and a fire was burning in the fireplace. I was warm from physical activity and sat near the table. You, on the other hand, had pulled a chair close to the fireplace. Just as I placed the parchment in your hand, and as you were examining it, Wolf, the Newfoundland dog, came in and jumped onto your shoulders. With your left hand you petted him and pushed him away, while your right hand, holding the parchment, dropped carelessly between your knees, very close to the fire. For a moment I thought the flames had caught it, and I was about to warn you, but before I could say anything, you had pulled it back and were studying it closely. When I thought about all these details, I had no doubt that heat had been what caused the skull design to appear on the parchment that I saw drawn on it. You know very well that chemical mixtures exist, and have existed since ancient times, that make it possible to write on either paper or parchment so that the letters only become visible when exposed to fire. Zaffre, dissolved in aqua regia and mixed with four times its weight in water, is sometimes used; this creates a green color. Cobalt regulus, dissolved in nitric acid, produces a red color. These colors fade after varying amounts of time once the material cools down, but become visible again when heat is applied once more."

I carefully examined the skull image. The outer edges of the drawing—those closest to the edge of the parchment—were much clearer than the rest. It was obvious that the heat had worked unevenly or incompletely. I immediately lit a fire and exposed every part of the parchment to intense heat. At first, the only result was that the faint lines of the skull became darker and more visible. However, as I continued the experiment, something appeared at the corner of the paper, diagonally across from where the skull was drawn—the outline of what I initially thought was a goat. Upon closer examination, though, I realized it was meant to be a young goat.

"Ha! ha!" I said, "I certainly have no right to laugh at you—a million and a half dollars is too serious a matter for amusement—but you're not about to establish a third link in your chain—you won't find any special connection between your pirates and a goat—pirates, you know, have nothing to do with goats; they belong to the farming business."

"But I just said that the figure wasn't that of a goat."

"Well, a kid then—pretty much the same thing."

"Pretty much, but not completely," Legrand replied. "You might have heard of a certain Captain Kidd. I immediately saw the figure of the animal as some sort of wordplay or symbolic signature. I call it a signature because where it was placed on the parchment gave me that impression. The skull and crossbones in the opposite diagonal corner looked like a stamp or official seal in the same way. But I was really frustrated by the lack of everything else—the main body of what I imagined was some kind of document—the actual text that would give meaning to my theory."

"I assume you were expecting to find a letter between the stamp and the signature."

"Something like that. The truth is, I felt overwhelmingly convinced that some incredible good fortune was about to happen. I can hardly explain why. Maybe it was more of a wish than a genuine belief—but you should know that Jupiter's foolish comments about the bug being made of pure gold had an extraordinary impact on my imagination. And then all those accidents and coincidences—they were absolutely remarkable. Do you notice how it was pure chance that these events happened on the only day of the entire year when it was cold enough to need a fire, and that without that fire, or without the dog showing up at exactly the right moment, I never would have discovered the skull, and therefore never would have found the treasure?"

"But go on—I'm completely eager to hear more."

"Well, you've certainly heard the many stories going around—the countless vague rumors floating about regarding money buried somewhere along the Atlantic coast by Kidd and his crew. These rumors must have some basis in reality. The fact that these rumors have persisted for so long and so consistently could only result, it seemed to me, from the circumstance that the buried treasure still remains buried. If Kidd had hidden his loot temporarily and later retrieved it, the rumors would hardly have reached us in their current unchanging form. You'll notice that all the stories told are about people searching for money, not about people finding money. If the pirate had recovered his treasure, the whole matter would have ended there. It appeared to me that some mishap—perhaps the loss of a note indicating its location—had stripped him of the ability to recover it, and that this mishap had become known to his followers, who otherwise might never have learned that treasure had been hidden at all, and who, engaging themselves in futile, because misdirected attempts to retrieve it, had first given birth to, and then widespread circulation to, the reports which are now so widespread. Have you ever heard of any significant treasure being discovered along the coast?"

"Never."

"But everyone knows that Kidd's treasure was enormous. I naturally assumed, therefore, that it was still buried somewhere; and you'll hardly be surprised when I tell you that I felt a hope, almost reaching certainty, that the parchment discovered in such a strange way contained a lost record of where the treasure was hidden."

"But how did you proceed?"

"I held the vellum up to the fire once more, making the flames burn hotter, but still nothing showed up. I began to think that the layer of grime covering it might be causing the problem, so I gently cleaned the parchment by pouring warm water over its surface. After doing this, I put it in a tin pan with the skull facing down and set the pan on top of a furnace filled with glowing charcoal. Within a few minutes, once the pan had heated up completely, I lifted out the slip of parchment and discovered, to my overwhelming delight, that it was marked in several spots with what looked like symbols arranged in rows. I put it back in the pan and let it stay there for another minute. When I took it out again, the entire thing looked exactly as you see it right now."

Here Legrand, after heating the parchment again, handed it to me for examination. The following characters were roughly drawn in red ink between the skull and the goat:

"53‡‡†305))6*;4826)4‡.)4‡);806*;48†8¶60))85;1‡(;:‡*8†
83(88)5*†;46(;88*96*?;8)*‡(;485);5*†2:*‡(;4956*2(5*—
4)8¶8*;4069285);)6†8)4‡‡;1(‡9;48081;8:8‡1;48†85;4)485†52
8806*81(‡9;48;(88;4(‡?34;48)4‡;161;:188;‡?;"

"But," I said, handing the slip back to him, "I'm still completely in the dark. Even if all the jewels of Golconda were waiting for me as a reward for solving this puzzle, I'm absolutely certain I wouldn't be able to earn them."

"And yet," said Legrand, "the solution isn't nearly as difficult as you might think from a quick first look at these symbols. Anyone could easily guess that these symbols form a code—meaning they carry a hidden message. But considering what we know about Kidd, I couldn't imagine he'd be capable of creating any of the more complex types of secret writing. I decided right away that this was a simple kind of code—the type that would seem completely impossible to solve to a sailor's basic understanding without having the key."

"And you really solved it?"

"Easily; I have solved others that were ten thousand times more complex. My circumstances and a particular way of thinking have led me to become interested in such puzzles, and it's questionable whether human cleverness can create a mystery of this type that human cleverness cannot solve through proper effort. In fact, once I had established connected and readable characters, I barely considered the simple difficulty of figuring out what they meant."

In this situation—and really in all cases involving secret codes—the first thing to consider is what language the cipher uses. The methods for solving codes, particularly the simpler ones, depend on and change based on the characteristics of the specific language being used. Usually, there's no choice but to try different languages through experimentation (guided by what seems most likely) among all the languages known to whoever is trying to solve it, until they find the correct one. However, with the cipher we're looking at now, all that difficulty disappeared because of the signature. The wordplay on "Kidd" only makes sense in English and no other language. Without this clue, I would have started my attempts with Spanish and French, since those are the languages a pirate from the Spanish Main would most likely have used to write this type of secret message. Given this evidence, I concluded that the cryptograph was written in English.

"You notice there are no spaces between the words. If there had been spaces, the job would have been relatively simple. In that situation, I would have started by comparing and examining the shorter words, and if a single-letter word had appeared, which is very likely (like 'a' or 'I,' for instance), I would have considered the puzzle solved. However, since there are no spaces, my initial step was to identify the most common letters as well as the rarest ones. After counting them all, I created a chart like this:"

Of the character 8 there are 33.

26.		
4	“	19..
	“	16.
*	“	13.
5	“	12.
6	“	11.
†1	“	8.
	“	6.
9.2	“	5.
.3	“	4.
	“	3.
	“	2.
“	1.	“

“In English, the letter that appears most often is e. After that, the order of frequency goes like this: a o i d h n r s t u y c f g l m w b k p q x z. The letter E is so dominant that you’ll rarely find a sentence of any reasonable length where it isn’t the most common character.”

“Here, then, we establish, right from the start, the foundation for something more than just a simple guess. The general purpose of this table is clear—but for this specific cipher, we’ll only need to use it partially. Since our most common character is 8, we’ll begin by assuming it represents the letter e in the regular alphabet. To confirm this assumption, let’s check if the 8 appears frequently in pairs—since e is doubled very often in English—in words like ‘meet,’ ‘fleet,’ ‘speed,’ ‘seen,’ ‘been,’ ‘agree,’ and so on. In this case, we can see it appears doubled no fewer than five times, even though the cryptograph is short.”

“Let’s assume 8, then, represents e. Now, among all words in the language, ‘the’ appears most frequently; let’s see, therefore, whether there are repetitions of any three characters, in the same order of arrangement, with the last one being 8. If we discover repetitions of such letters, arranged this way, they will most likely represent the word 'the.' Upon examination, we find no fewer than seven such arrangements, the characters being ;48. We may, therefore, assume that ; represents t, 4 represents h, and 8 represents e—the last being now well confirmed. Thus a significant step has been taken.

"But, having established a single word, we can now establish a vastly important point; that is to say, several beginnings and endings of other words. Let us look, for example, at the second-to-last instance in which the combination ;48 appears—not far from the end of the cipher. We know that the ; immediately following is the beginning of a word, and, of the six characters that come after this 'the,' we know no less than five. Let us write these characters down, using the letters we know they represent, leaving a space for the unknown—teeth.

"Here we can immediately eliminate the 'th,' since it doesn't form part of the word that begins with the first t; by testing every letter of the alphabet to fill the empty space, we discover that no word can be created where this th would be a component. This narrows our options to"

t ee,

and, going through the alphabet if needed, just as we did before, we reach the word 'tree' as the only possible interpretation. This gives us another letter, r, shown by the symbol (, with the words 'the tree' placed side by side.

Looking past these words for a brief span, we once again encounter the combination ;48, and we use it as an ending to what comes directly before. This gives us the following arrangement:

the tree; the,

or, replacing the natural letters where they are known, it reads as follows:

the tree through the.

"Now, if we replace the unknown characters with blank spaces or substitute dots instead, we read it like this:"

the tree through the,

when the word 'through' becomes immediately apparent. However, this discovery provides us with three additional letters, o, u and g, represented by ‡, ? and 3.

"Looking closely now through the cipher for combinations of familiar characters, we discover, not very far from the beginning, this arrangement,"

83(88, or egree,

which clearly shows us the ending of the word 'degree,' and provides us with another letter, d, represented by †.

"Four letters after the word 'degree,' we see the combination

;46(;88.

"Translating the known characters, and representing the unknown by dots, as before, we read thus:"

I notice the text "th.rtee," appears to be incomplete or corrupted. Could you please provide the complete heading you'd like me to rewrite? This fragment doesn't contain enough information for me to understand what it's meant to say.

an arrangement that immediately brings to mind the word 'thirteen,' and once again providing us with two new characters, i and n, represented by 6 and *.

"Looking now at the start of the cryptograph, we discover the combination,

53‡‡†.

"Following the same translation method as before, we get"

good,

which confirms that the first letter is A, and that the first two words are 'A good.'

"It's now time for us to organize our key, as far as we've discovered it, in a table format to prevent confusion. It will appear like this:"

5 represents a

†	"	d
8	"	e
3	"	g
4	"	h
6	"	i
*	"	n
‡	"	o

"We have, therefore, no less than eleven of the most important letters represented, and it will be unnecessary to proceed with the details of the solution. I have said enough to convince you that ciphers of this nature are readily solvable, and to give you some insight into the reasoning behind their development. But be assured that the specimen before us belongs to the very simplest type of cryptograph. It now only remains to give you the full translation of the characters upon the parchment, as decoded. Here it is:"

"'A good glass in the bishop's hostel in the devil's seat forty-one degrees and thirteen minutes northeast and by north main branch seventh limb east side shoot from the left eye of the death's-head a bee line from the tree through the shot fifty feet out.'"

"But," I said, "the puzzle still seems just as confusing as before. How can we possibly figure out what all this nonsense about 'devil's seats,' 'death's heads,' and 'bishop's hotels' means?"

"I admit," Legrand responded, "that the situation still appears quite serious when you take a quick look at it. My initial effort was to break down the sentence into the natural sections that the code-maker intended."

"You mean, to punctuate it?"

"Something like that."

"But how could this be accomplished?"

"I realized that the writer had deliberately run his words together without any breaks, making the puzzle much harder to solve. When someone who isn't particularly clever tries to do this, they almost always go too far with it. During his writing, whenever he reached a natural break in his message that would normally call for a pause or punctuation mark, he would likely squeeze his letters even closer together than usual at that spot. If you examine the manuscript carefully, you'll notice five places where the letters are unusually crowded together. Using this observation as my guide, I divided the text like this: 'A good glass in the Bishop's hostel in the Devil's seat—forty-one degrees and thirteen minutes—northeast and by north—main branch seventh limb east side—shoot from the left eye of the death's-head—a bee-line from the tree through the shot fifty feet out."'

"Even this explanation," I said, "still leaves me confused."

"It left me just as confused," Legrand replied, "for several days. During that time, I searched thoroughly around Sullivan's Island, looking for any building called the 'Bishop's Hotel.' I had naturally updated the old-fashioned word 'hostel' to something more modern. When I couldn't find any information about it, I was about to expand my search area and approach it more systematically. Then one morning, it suddenly occurred to me that this 'Bishop's

Hostel' might be connected to an old family named Bessop, who had owned an ancient manor house about four miles north of the island for as long as anyone could remember. So I went to the plantation and started asking questions again, this time focusing on the older Black residents there. Eventually, one of the eldest women told me she had heard of a place called Bessop's Castle. She thought she could show me where it was, but she explained that it wasn't actually a castle or an inn—it was a tall rock formation."

"I offered to pay her generously for her efforts, and after some hesitation, she agreed to come with me to the location. We located it without too much trouble, and after sending her away, I began to examine the area. The 'castle' was made up of a random collection of cliffs and rocks—one of them particularly striking for both its towering height and its isolated, man-made appearance. I climbed to the top, and then found myself uncertain about what to do next."

While I was deep in thought, I noticed a narrow ledge on the eastern side of the rock, roughly a yard below where I was standing. This ledge stuck out about eighteen inches and was no more than a foot wide, while a hollow space in the cliff directly above it made it look somewhat like one of those high-backed chairs our ancestors used to sit in. I felt certain that this was the 'devil's seat' mentioned in the manuscript, and suddenly I felt like I understood the complete solution to the puzzle.

"The 'good glass,' I realized, could only refer to a telescope, since sailors rarely use the word 'glass' to mean anything else. I immediately understood that this was a telescope meant to be used from a specific, unchanging viewpoint. I didn't doubt that the phrases 'forty-one degrees and thirteen minutes' and 'northeast and by north' were meant as instructions for positioning the telescope. Thrilled by these discoveries, I rushed home, got a telescope, and came back to the rock."

I lowered myself down to the ledge and discovered that it was impossible to maintain a stable position on it except in one specific spot. This observation confirmed what I had already suspected. I began to use the telescope. Obviously, the "forty-one degrees and thirteen minutes" could only refer to the angle of elevation above the visible horizon, since the horizontal direction was clearly specified by the phrase "northeast and by north." I immediately determined this direction using a pocket compass; then, aiming the telescope at approximately a forty-one-degree angle of elevation as accurately as I could estimate, I carefully adjusted it up and down until something caught my attention—a circular gap or opening in the leaves of a large tree that towered above the others in the distance. In the center of this opening, I noticed a white object, though I couldn't initially identify what it was. After adjusting the telescope's focus, I looked again and realized it was a human skull.

"After making this discovery, I became so confident that I believed the mystery was solved; the phrase 'main branch, seventh limb, east side' could only refer to where the skull was positioned on the tree, while 'shoot from the left eye of the death's head' also had just one possible meaning when it came to searching for buried treasure. I realized that the plan was to drop a bullet from the left eye of the skull, and that a direct line—or in other words, a straight line—drawn from the closest point of the trunk through 'the shot' (or the spot where the bullet landed) and then extended fifty feet further, would point to a specific location—and I thought it was quite possible that something valuable was buried beneath that spot."

"All of this," I said, "is extremely clear, and while clever, it's still straightforward and easy to understand. When you left the Bishop's Hotel, what happened next?"

"So, after carefully noting the position of the tree, I headed back home. The moment I stepped away from 'the devil's seat,' though, the circular opening disappeared completely; I couldn't catch sight of it again no matter how I tried to position myself. What strikes me as the most clever aspect of this entire situation is the reality (since multiple tests have proven to me that it's true) that this circular gap can only be seen from one specific vantage point—the narrow shelf on the rock face itself.

"On this trip to the 'Bishop's Hotel,' Jupiter had come with me. He had undoubtedly noticed over the past several weeks how distracted I had been acting, and he made sure not to leave me by myself. However, the following day, I got up very early and managed to sneak away from him, then headed into the hills to look for the tree. After a great deal of hard work, I discovered it. When I returned home that evening, my servant threatened to give me a beating. As for the rest of what happened, I believe you know the story just as well as I do."

"I suppose," I said, "you missed the spot on your first attempt at digging because Jupiter made the mistake of dropping the bug through the right eye of the skull instead of through the left eye."

"Exactly. This error created a difference of roughly two and a half inches in the 'shot'—meaning the position of the peg closest to the tree. If the treasure had been buried directly under the 'shot,' this mistake wouldn't have mattered much. However, the 'shot' and the nearest point of the tree served only as reference points to establish a directional line. Naturally, even though the error seemed minor at first, it grew larger as we followed the line further. By the time we had traveled fifty feet, it had completely thrown us off track. If I hadn't been so firmly convinced that treasure was actually buried somewhere in this area, we might have wasted all our effort for nothing."

"But your fancy way of speaking, and how you acted when swinging that beetle around—it was incredibly strange! I was convinced you had lost your mind. And why did you insist on dropping the bug from the skull instead of using a bullet?"

"To be honest, I was somewhat irritated by your obvious doubts about my mental state, so I decided to quietly get back at you in my own way through a bit of deliberate mystery. That's why I swung the beetle around, and that's why I dropped it from the tree. Your comment about how heavy it was gave me the idea for the latter."

"Yes, I understand; and now there's only one thing that confuses me. What should we make of the skeletons found in the hole?"

"That's a question I can't answer any better than you can. However, there seems to be only one believable explanation for them—though it's horrible to accept the kind of brutality my theory would suggest. It's obvious that Kidd—assuming Kidd really did hide this treasure, which I'm sure he did—it's clear he must have had help with the work. But once the job was finished, he might have decided it was wise to eliminate everyone who knew his secret. Maybe a couple of strikes with a pickaxe did the job while his helpers were still working in the pit; maybe it took a dozen blows—who can say?"

Four Beasts In One—The Homo-Cameleopard

Everyone has their own virtues.

—Crébillon's Xerxes.

Antiochus Epiphanes is widely regarded as the Gog mentioned by the prophet Ezekiel. However, this distinction more accurately belongs to Cambyses, the son of Cyrus. The Syrian monarch's character certainly doesn't require any additional dramatic flourishes. His rise to power, or more accurately his seizure of the throne, occurred one hundred and seventy-one years before Christ's arrival. His attempt to rob the temple of Diana at Ephesus, his relentless hatred toward the Jews, his desecration of the Holy of Holies, and his wretched death at Taba following a chaotic eleven-year reign represent the most notable events of his rule. These major incidents received far more attention from contemporary historians than the godless, cowardly, brutal, foolish, and erratic acts that characterized his personal life and shaped his overall reputation.

Let us imagine, dear reader, that it is now the year 3830, and let us, for a few minutes, picture ourselves at that most bizarre dwelling place of humanity, the extraordinary city of Antioch. Certainly there were, in Syria and other regions, sixteen cities with that name, in addition to the one I am specifically referring to. But ours is the one that was known as Antiochia Epidaphne, named for its closeness to the small village of Daphne, where a temple to that god stood. It was constructed (though there is some disagreement about this) by Seleucus Nicanor, the first ruler of the region after Alexander the Great, in honor of his father Antiochus, and immediately became the home of the Syrian royal family. During the prosperous era of the Roman Empire, it served as the regular headquarters of the governor of the eastern territories; and many of the emperors of the imperial city (among whom we should mention, particularly, Verus and Valens) lived here for most of their lives. But I notice we have reached the city itself. Let us climb this fortress wall, and cast our gaze upon the town and surrounding countryside.

"What is that wide and fast-flowing river that pushes its way through countless waterfalls across the mountainous wilderness, and eventually through the wilderness of buildings?"

That is the Orontes, and it's the only water visible, except for the Mediterranean, which spreads like a vast mirror about twelve miles to the south. Everyone has seen the Mediterranean; but let me tell you, there are few who have caught a glimpse of Antioch. By few, I mean those who, like you and me, have enjoyed the benefits of a modern education at the same time. So stop looking at that sea, and focus entirely on the cluster of buildings spread out below us. You'll recall that this is now the year of the world three thousand eight hundred and thirty. If it were later—say, if it were the year of our Lord eighteen hundred and forty-five, we would miss this remarkable sight. In the nineteenth century Antioch is—that is to say, Antioch will be—in a pitiful state of ruin. By that time, it will have been completely destroyed on three separate occasions by three consecutive earthquakes. In fact, to be honest, whatever little remains of its former glory will be found in such a desolate and crumbling condition that the patriarch will have moved his residence to Damascus. This is good. I see you're taking my advice and making the most of your time examining the place—in

—satisfying your eyes
With the monuments and the famous sights
That bring the most renown to this city.—

I apologize; I had forgotten that Shakespeare won't emerge for another seventeen hundred and fifty years. But doesn't the appearance of Epidaphne justify my calling it grotesque?

"It is well fortified; and in this respect is as much indebted to nature as to art."

Very true.

"There are an enormous number of magnificent palaces."

There are.

"And the many temples, luxurious and magnificent, can be compared with the most praised ones from ancient times."

I have to admit all of this is true. Yet there are countless mud huts and terrible shacks everywhere. We can't help but notice the overwhelming amount of filth in every gutter, and if it weren't for the overpowering smell of religious incense, I'm certain we would encounter an absolutely unbearable stench. Have you ever seen streets so impossibly narrow, or buildings so incredibly tall? What darkness their shadows throw across the ground! It's fortunate that the hanging lamps in those never-ending covered walkways are kept lit all day long; otherwise we would experience the darkness of Egypt during the time of its destruction.

"This is definitely a strange place! What does that unusual building over there mean? Look! It rises above all the other buildings and sits to the east of what I believe is the royal palace!"

That is the new Temple of the Sun, which is worshipped in Syria under the name Elah Gabalah. In the future, a very infamous Roman Emperor will bring this worship to Rome and take his name from it, becoming known as Heliogabalus. I'm sure you would like to catch a glimpse of the god of this temple. You don't need to look up at the sky; his divine presence isn't there—at least not the version of the sun god that the Syrians worship. That deity can be found inside that building over there. He is worshipped in the form of a large stone pillar that ends at the top in a cone or pyramid shape, which represents Fire.

"Listen—look!—who could those ridiculous people be, half naked, with their faces painted, shouting and gesturing to the crowd?"

A few are charlatans. Others belong more specifically to the class of philosophers. The largest group, however—particularly those who beat the common people with clubs—are the king's chief courtiers, dutifully carrying out some praiseworthy comedy devised by the monarch.

"But what do we have here? Good heavens! The town is overrun with wild animals! What a terrifying sight!—what a dangerous situation!"

Frightening, if you will; but not dangerous in the slightest. Each animal, if you take the time to watch, follows very calmly behind its owner. A few, certainly, are led with a rope around the neck, but these are mainly the smaller or more fearful types. The lion, the tiger, and the leopard move completely free. They have been easily trained for their current work, and serve their individual masters as personal attendants. It is true, there are times when Nature reclaims her violated territory;—but then the devouring of a soldier, or the strangling of a sacred bull, is a matter of too little importance to be more than mentioned in passing in Epidaphne.

"But what incredible uproar do I hear? This is certainly loud noise even for Antioch! It suggests some disturbance of unusual significance."

Yes—absolutely. The king has commanded some new spectacle—some gladiatorial show at the hippodrome—or perhaps the slaughter of the Scythian prisoners—or the burning of his new palace—or the demolition of a beautiful temple—or, indeed, a bonfire of a few Jews. The commotion grows louder. Bursts of laughter rise to the heavens. The air becomes harsh with wind instruments, and terrible with the clamor of a million voices. Let us go down, for the sake of entertainment, and see what is happening! This way—watch out! Here we are on the main street, which is called the street of Timarchus. The sea of people is moving this way, and we will have trouble going against the current. They are flooding through the alley of Heraclides, which leads straight from the palace;—therefore the king is most likely among the crowd. Yes—I hear the shouts of the herald announcing his approach in the grand language of the East. We will catch a glimpse of him as he passes by the temple of Ashimah. Let us hide ourselves in the entrance of the sanctuary; he will be here soon. In the meantime let us examine this statue. What is it? Oh! it is the god Ashimah himself. You notice, however, that he is neither a lamb, nor a goat, nor a satyr, nor does he bear much resemblance to the Pan of the Arcadians. Yet all these forms have been attributed—I beg pardon—will be attributed—by the scholars of future ages, to the Ashimah of the Syrians. Put on your spectacles, and tell me what it is. What is it?

"Good heavens! It's an ape!"

True—a baboon; but still very much a god. His name comes from the Greek word Simia—what complete idiots these scholars of ancient history are! But look!—look!—over there runs a scruffy little street kid. Where is he headed? What is he shouting about? What is he saying? Oh! he says the king is arriving in victory; that he is dressed in his royal robes; that he has just finished killing, with his own hands, a thousand chained Israelite prisoners! For this achievement the little rascal is praising him to the heavens! Listen! here comes a group of similar people. They have written a Latin hymn about the king's bravery, and are singing it as they walk:

Thousands, thousands, thousands,
Thousands, thousands, thousands,
We have beheaded, one man!
Thousands, thousands, thousands, thousands,
we have beheaded!
Thousands, thousands, thousands,
Long live he who has killed thousands upon thousands!
No one has as much wine
As the blood he has spilled!(*1)

Which can be explained this way:

A thousand, a thousand, a thousand,
A thousand, a thousand, a thousand,
We, with one warrior, have killed!
A thousand, a thousand, a thousand, a thousand.
Sing a thousand once more!
Hooray!—let us sing
Long life to our king,
Who defeated a thousand so splendid!
Hooray!—let us shout,

He has given us more
Red gallons of blood
Than all Syria can provide of wine!

"Do you hear that flourish of trumpets?"

Yes—the king is coming! Look! The people are stunned with awe, and they raise their eyes to the heavens in reverence. He comes!—he is coming!—there he is!

"Who?—where?—the king?—I don't see him—I can't say that I notice him."

Then you must be blind.

"Very possible. Still I see nothing but a chaotic crowd of fools and lunatics, who are busy throwing themselves down before a gigantic giraffe, and trying to get a kiss from the animal's hooves. Look! the beast has very rightfully kicked one of the mob over—and another—and another—and another. Indeed, I cannot help admiring the animal for the excellent use he is making of his feet."

Rabble, you say!—but these are the noble and free citizens of Epidaphne! Beasts, you called them?—be careful that no one overhears you. Don't you see that the animal has a human face? Why, my dear fellow, that giraffe is none other than Antiochus Epiphanes, Antiochus the Illustrious, King of Syria, and the most powerful of all the rulers of the East! It's true that he's sometimes called Antiochus Epimanes—Antiochus the madman—but that's only because not everyone has the ability to recognize his greatness. It's also true that he's currently wrapped in an animal's hide and doing his best to act like a giraffe; but he's doing this to better maintain his royal dignity. Besides, the king is enormous in size, so the costume is neither inappropriate nor too large for him. We can assume, however, that he wouldn't have put it on except for some particularly important state occasion. Such an occasion, you'll agree, is the slaughter of a thousand Jews. With what superior dignity the monarch walks around on all fours! His tail, you'll notice, is held high by his two chief mistresses, Elline and Argelais; and his entire appearance would be infinitely impressive, if not for his bulging eyes, which look ready to pop out of his head, and the strange color of his face, which has become impossible to describe from the amount of wine he's consumed. Let's follow him to the hippodrome, where he's heading, and listen to the victory song he's beginning to sing:

Who is king but Epiphanes?
Tell me—do you know?
Who is king but Epiphanes?
Excellent!—excellent!
There is no one but Epiphanes,
No—there is no one:
So tear down the temples,
And extinguish the sun!

Excellently and powerfully performed! The crowd is calling him 'Prince of Poets,' along with 'Glory of the East,' 'Delight of the Universe,' and 'Most Extraordinary of Giraffes.' They have demanded an encore of his performance, and can you hear?—he is singing it once more. When he reaches the hippodrome, he will receive the poetic crown, in expectation of his triumph at the upcoming Olympics.

"But, good Jupiter! what is happening in the crowd behind us?"

Behind us, did you say?—oh! ah!—I see. My friend, it's good that you spoke when you did. Let's get to a safe place as quickly as possible. Here!—let's hide ourselves in the arch of this aqueduct, and I'll tell you shortly about what started this commotion. It has turned out just as I expected. The strange appearance of the cameleopard with a man's head has, it seems, offended the sense of decency held, in general, by the wild animals kept domesticated in the city. A rebellion has been the result; and, as is usual on such occasions, all human efforts will be useless in controlling the mob. Several of the Syrians have already been eaten; but the general opinion of the four-footed patriots seems to be in favor of devouring the cameleopard. 'The Prince of Poets,' therefore, is up on his hind legs, running for his life. His courtiers have abandoned him, and his concubines have followed such an excellent example. 'Delight of the Universe,' you are in a terrible situation! 'Glory of the East,' you are in danger of being chewed up! Therefore don't worry so pitifully about your tail; it will certainly be dragged through the mud, and there's nothing that can be done about this. Don't look behind you, then, at its inevitable disgrace; but take courage, move your legs with energy, and race for the hippodrome! Remember that you are Antiochus Epiphanes. Antiochus the Illustrious!—also 'Prince of Poets,' 'Glory of the East,' 'Delight of the Universe,' and 'Most Remarkable of Cameleopards!' Heavens! what incredible speed you are showing! What amazing ability to escape you are demonstrating! Run, Prince!—Bravo, Epiphanes! Well done, Cameleopard!—Glorious Antiochus!—He runs!—he leaps!—he flies! Like an arrow from a catapult he approaches the hippodrome! He leaps!—he shrieks!—he is there! This is good; for if you, 'Glory of the East,' had been half a second longer in reaching the gates of the Amphitheatre, there isn't a bear cub in Epidaphne that wouldn't have taken a bite at your body. Let's get out of here—let's leave!—because we'll find our sensitive modern ears unable to bear the tremendous noise which is about to begin in celebration of the king's escape! Listen! it has already started. Look!—the whole town is in chaos.

"This must be the most crowded city in the East! What a sea of people! What a mix of every social class and age group! What a multitude of religious groups and nationalities! What a range of clothing styles! What a tower of Babel of languages! What a roaring of animals! What a chiming of instruments! What a bunch of philosophers!"

Come, let's go.

"Wait a moment! I see a huge commotion in the hippodrome; what does it mean, I ask you?"

That?—oh, it's nothing! The noble and free citizens of Epidaphne, being completely convinced of their king's faith, courage, wisdom, and divine nature, and having personally witnessed his recent extraordinary athletic ability, believe it's only right to place upon his head (along with the poetic crown) the victory wreath from the footrace—a wreath that he's clearly destined to win at the upcoming Olympic games, and which they're therefore presenting to him now in anticipation.

THE END

Thank You For Reading

You've Just Read a Piece of the Greatest Library Ever Rebuilt

Thank you for reading.

This book is one of thousands we're restoring, reimagining, and translating as part of the **Modern Library of Alexandria** — a global movement to preserve and share humanity's most important ideas.

What was once lost to fire and time is now rising again — not just as memory, but as living, breathing knowledge, freely accessible to all.

What You Can Do Next:

- **Keep Reading.**

  Discover more legendary works — in beautiful print, audiobook, or digital form — at LibraryofAlexandria.com.

- **Build Your Own Library.**

  Every title is available as a paperback, hardcover, or collectible boxset — at true printing cost. Craft a personal library worthy of display.

- **Spread the Light.**

  Share this book. Tell others about the movement. Help us translate every timeless work into every language, so no reader is ever left behind.

By finishing this book, you've already taken part in something extraordinary.

Join us at LibraryofAlexandria.com

Together, we're rebuilding the greatest library the world has ever known.

With appreciation,

The Modern Library of Alexandria Team

Visit:
www.libraryofalexandria.com
Or scan the code below:

www.ingramcontent.com/pod-product-compliance
Lightning Source LLC
Chambersburg PA
CBHW011525240626
47154CB00009B/2977
* 9 7 8 1 8 0 6 6 8 0 4 8 1 *